UNCIVILIZED

ISBN : 978-1-4467-2022-6

Uncivilized

Five short essays by

Artxmis Graham Thoreau

***

Edited by Lothric Wildman

The author :

Artxmis Graham Thoreau is an anarchist from the Midwest with a deep love for the Wild. Former contributor to Oak Journal, Artxmis is one of the two individuals behind the Uncivilized Project which encompasses the Uncivilized Podcast and Uncivilized Distro. The introductory text of the project specifying, among other things, that

« Where others either adopt the anarchist Utopian image or reject the label entirely, we seek a middle way — to make anarchism a praxis that is anti-political *and* anti-technology. We believe one cannot be an anarchist and not reject technology. As others such as Ellul, Perlman and Kaczynski have shown: personal and local autonomy is *not* compatible with technology. We are Luddites, Primitivists, Anti-Civilizationists and Post-Civilizationists. We are Nihilists, Egoists and Materialists ».

He is also currently contributing to the upcoming publication *Plastic in Utero: a journal of anti-civ anarchy.*

Contents

*

Collapse: Observations and Predictions

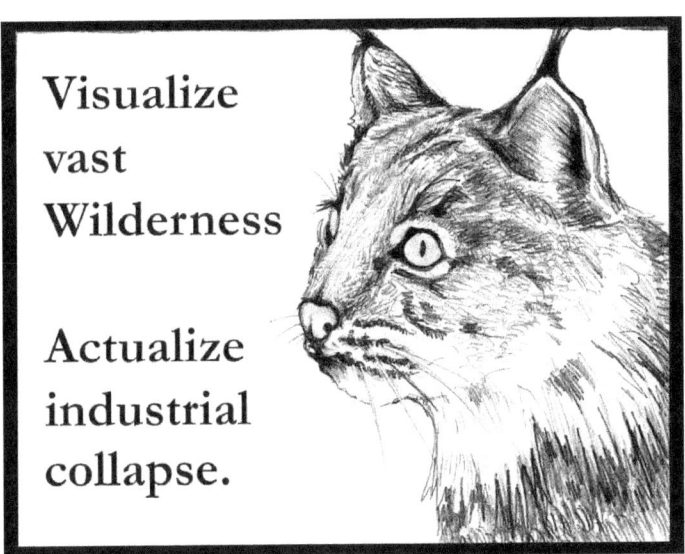

Visualize vast Wilderness

Actualize industrial collapse.

Collapse?

The 'Collapse' is a term employed by the whole of the political spectrum, from communists referring to the collapse of capitalism, to right-wing celebrations for the collapse of the Soviet Union. Unlike aforementioned political groups, 'Collapse' has come to define entirely different things for Luddites, Primitivists, and movements alike. The 'Collapse' is an observation, and a prediction to the degradation of world society.

As stated, it is both an *observation* and a *prediction*. What does this mean? It means the Collapse is happening now, and if we stay on our current course, it is within the realm of possibility that it is inevitable.

Before we expand, we should further define 'Collapse'. A rough and offhand definition can be written as:

Either a long-term or short-term degradation of major systems of organization (states; governments; economic systems; and in our case, World Society) *that eventually leads to a total withering or restructuring of said systems that primarily represents itself in political and/or social upheaval and disillusionment. Usually violent in cause and/or consequences.*

Such visions of Collapse can be pulled from major anti-tech writers, such as the likes of Kaczynski:

The aim of the Freedom Club is the complete and permanent destruction of modern industrial society in every part of the world. This means no more airplanes, no more radios, no more miracle drugs, no more paved roads, and so forth.

Observations

A prevalent example of our observations is the anti-globalization movement that spanned from the 80's to the early 2000's. It was a widely spread movement, ranging from communists and socialists, to primitivists and neo-nazi movements. Such cases would be the Paris 89 protests (July 1989), WTO protests in Seattle (Nov 30, 1999) and the 27th G8 Summit Protests (July, 2001).

What are the implications of such a movement? Obviously, the movement has died off and replaced almost entirely by alt-globalization pushed solely by leftist types. However, there is light at the end of the tunnel, because it proved that people will not blindly accept a future in which their personal and local lives will be dictated by elites *(however, one failing of the movement was a lack of a strong definition of who these elites were — Bankers? Jews? Capitalists? Technicians?).*

It also proved that it was not necessarily a political movement in a traditional sense, rather, a social movement. It spread across so many ideologies and tendencies that it showed a HUMAN drive, not purely classist or political. This of course, calls back to Jacques Camatte's idea, that the true revolution would not be a class war, but a war of humanity against domestication and capital (i.e. primal war).

Yet another observation is that Collapse is a contemporary phenomenon, proven by the re-emerging interest in Primitivism, through writers such as Zerzan, Kaczynski and Jacobi.

In August of 2017, *Discovery* aired their first episode of *Manhunt: Unabomber,* a dramatized look into Kaczynski's life and theories. This brought on a whole reemergence of his thought, as explained in Jake Hanrahan's *Inside the Unabomber's odd and furious online revival,* where he explored the 'ironic' rise of internet interest in Kaczynski's theories. (**NOTE: The subjects of the article are commonly associated with so-called « eco-fascist » ideology, less so with mainstream primitivism or neo-luddism).**

John H. Richarson also has written on the topic of anti-tech movements, publishing a lengthy, and in-depth analysis of Kaczynskian movements, individuals and the consequences of it all in *New York Magazine.* It mainly features John Jacobi, but delves into movements and individuals surrounding them, such as Deep Green Resistance (DGR), Individualists Tending Towards the Wild (ITS, now Wild Reaction) and so on.

In addition, ecological devastation has been common in popular discussion because of new findings, publications and demands of climate science panels such as IPCC's report. With post-industrial behavior, we are expected to reach an increase of 1.5 °C / 2.7° F above pre-industrial levels in the coming decades. To put this in perspective, the report stated that by 2017, *human induced change* had caused an increase of 1°C.

Of course, IPCC states the world's nations must come together to stop this destructive behavior, and instead we have seen an increase of emissions in 2018. On the other hand, several nations have indeed pushed to reduce carbon and other emissions in coming years, as well as other policies, such as cutting plastic waste.

Predictions

The fact of the matter is that there has yet to be a global social movement to stop the effects of techno-industrialism, that does not also pull into question the existence of the system. Why? Because the two cannot exist together. To make a stand against these behaviors, one must be critical towards World Society and large-scale organizational technologies.

Our predictions stem from these facts of recent history and also contemporary phenomena. We see the questioning of World Society has been a social, human movement, and that with the rise of ecological devastation* (and systematic opposition to fixing such problems) we can deduce that such a movement congruent to the anti-globalization movement is then possible.

In fact, people like Jacobi[1] predict such a movement to be an international *populist* movement:

"It's very likely that some form of anti-technology populism is going to replace what was once an anti-government populism; whereas the main objects of disdain were once politicians, the new objects of disdain will be scientists and engineers, as well as technology itself."

*This is not to say it will be focused on ecological devastation, but the accelerated devastation of our planet must necessarily accelerate social and political actions, if there are to be any at all.

Aha! Natural Collapse!

The question naturally arises then: Should we simply rely on a natural collapse? (Naturally meaning without human influence.)

My answer is **no**. I say this only because the safety nets around modern civilization are so advanced, and are becoming greater and greater, and we should not praise the Collapse like the Book of Revelation, with us then hoping for the best!

However, a Collapse is, on this course, *unavoidable-* not meaning ecological collapse will directly cause civilizational collapse, but that a rise in stresses in society will lead to a movement against the system itself. The only way it can be avoided is that:

1. Genetic engineering surpasses and overtakes human freewill. (See "Control of Human Behavior" in *Industrial Society and Its Future*.)

---

[1] *[Editor's Note]* John Jacobi is a neo-Luddite and environmentalist writer. Ideologically inspired by Ted Kaczynski, he published the magazines *The Wildernist* and *Hunter/Gatherer*, and also founded The Wildist Institute. He recently wrote the book *Repent to the Primitive –* that I have just republished, in which he presents a philosophical reflection about rewilding.

2. Pass into a stage of human development in which humans and all other life and aspects of Earth are fully assimilated. (Possibly linked to A, but also possible through "Fully Automated Luxury Communism")
3. Replacement of Man by a superior system such as AI. (See the second chapter of Ted's *Anti-Tech Revolution: Why and How.*)

To clarify, I am NOT saying a natural collapse is not possible, I am saying it should NOT be seen as a solution to our problems, or as an excuse for laziness on the behalf of "revolutionaries".

Conclusion

With the rise of primitivism and skepticism on technology, and the furthering ecological devastation (and the two are definitely linked!) we can expect, or in the least, hope for a populist, social movement against world society, similar to the anti-globalization movement.

Keep in mind, not to treat this as communists do, praising their « Proletarian Revolution » in a biblical light. Our movement, the Collapse is *now* and we should see ourselves actualizing it, operating alongside this phenomenon to accelerate industrial collapse.

***

Towards a New Anti-Technological Cause

Forward

The ideas put forth are not meant to be original. Many readers may claim most of the ideas such as the critique of Leftism is simply a reduced carbon-copy of Kaczynski's *Industrial Society and Its Future*. This is largely true. The purpose of this work is to condense the ideas from Kaczynski and others into a more layman-friendly, print-out friendly piece. It is also a critique of 'Neo-Luddism', which I haven't found outside of Techie criticisms.

In addition, the ideology presented below is a synthesis of philosophical anarchism or political nihilism, anarcho-primitivism and Kaczynski's own anti-tech ideas. Thus, one may see a large collection of varying ideas. Eclectic is a term to use here.

For Wildness,

A.G. T.

Introduction

From the actions of the quasi-labor movements of the 19th century Luddites, to the 1970's-1990's radical anti-tech campaign of Theodore Kaczynski and the deceased anti-globalization movement; skepticism of the *myth of progress* has been present in the last few hundred years.

This skepticism has developed alongside the development of Industrial technologies such as mass communication and transportation, as well as surveillance systems and advanced weapons.

Now, as we are reaching a tipping-point of environmental sustainability and mass violence, the 'luddite' movement can be argued to have stagnated. It has maintained reformist attitudes, concerned more with liberal environmental issues and socialist-labor rhetoric. This is Neo-Luddism.

Such a source of these attitudes is Chellis Glendinning's *Notes toward a Neo-Luddite Manifesto,* published in 1990. The content is a fair analysis of the reality of the old Luddite's goals: concerned more with "hurtful" technology and free-market capitalism. In addition, Glendinning puts forth a program in which technologies of our time should be rejected: television; nuclear, chemical, genetic, electro-magnetic and computer technologies.

I agree these technologies should be rejected, but this shows Glendinning and the old Luddites were concerned more with *certain* technologies rather than the basis of the larger issues themselves: the whole of the present technological and economic system of their (and our) time.

The reality is, we must object, in a revolutionary manner, all Industrial technologies. Such a view means a break with 'Neo-Luddism'. Neo-Luddites are again, reformists and labor activists. The Social Democrats of technology.

A New Ideology

Anti-Technology (Anti-Technologist, Anti-Tech) is a reaction to two main components of society: the basis of present society, technological and economic advances (the totality of modern civilization) and the failed reactions to it. Such failed reactions are anarcho-primitivism, neo-luddism and radical environmentalism.

If Anti-Tech shares ideas with these groups, what are those ideas?

Anti-Technology rejects technology for reasons such as the centralization of power into the hands of a technocratic class (beyond the bourgeoisie), environmental degradation, the removal of individual and small group autonomy and dignity.

The details have been laid out from works of individuals such as Jacques Ellul, Theodore Kaczynski, Edward Abbey and organizations such as the ELF and the early *Earth First!* movement.

Unlike Neo-Luddism, Anti-Tech rejects *all* technology, in the sense of industrial technologies. Many within AP would like a total return to a non-civilized way of life, but such a goal is idealistic, as after the collapse of world-wide industry, history will not be guided by revolutionaries.

As such, Anti-Tech creates a revolutionary value system based on the rejection of industrial technology, and the exalting of ecological systems outside of systematic human control (Wild Nature), community, self-reliance and dignity.

This is where the largest divide of Anti-Technology and Neo-Luddism is. The Neo-Luddites want to keep industrial society within a framework, based on communal and organic design.

Anti-Tech, however, wishes to see a sort of 'collapse' of techno-industrialism, meaning all technologies based on the principles and developments from the Industrial Revolution, on a global scale.

Anti-Technologists should question the legitimacy of the state, morality, ideology and mass-economics, all in addition to the core critique of techno-industrial society and civilization.

This is because we push for the highest state of personal autonomy, or in the least, giving people a chance to find it. Post-Collapse, the power of states, churches and other large institutions will be severely weakened.

We can be described as anarchists, populists, nihilists, primitivists (in the general use of the term) but people will choose to use or not to use these secondary-labels, as Anti-Technologist should come first. (For example, the author of this uses all previously listed labels as complementary to Anti-Tech.)

Activism or Revolution?

Despite the similar surface-level goals of Anarcho-Primitivism (AP) and Anti-Tech, AP is concerned more with non-revolutionary politics. It is a programme for activism, for the sake of activism. It has more in common with political Leftism than a truly revolutionary movement that seeks the goals AP *claims* to uphold. In fact, it more concerned with these ideas than the collapse of industry or civilization!

Political Leftism, in the Western sense, is a programme of activism: gay rights, animal rights, women's rights and other such movements. Interestingly, many leftists do *not* fit into these groups, and seek to 'protect' them. They align with these groups as long as it is in their political interests.

Should a gay-man not align with a Leftist, the Leftist becomes frustrated, because in their eyes, the gay-man belongs to their movement. He is a token marginalized person of the Left. The Leftist does not believe the gay-man can help himself.

When a marginalized person or group does not align with Leftism, or specific Leftist movements (say, Marxism-Leninism), the Leftist will become hostile and reject that individual or group. They may call them Uncle-Toms or self-hating, when in reality, the Leftist is self-hating, or hating of others.

Activism for the sake of activism, best put as reformism (usually social or basic economic reforms such as gay marriage and universal healthcare), takes away from revolutionary potential. Some may argue it serves as a breeding pool of revolutionary potential and values, but this is uncommon at best and ahistorical at worst. For example, the Bolsevhik's reformist policies came from pre-developed revolutionary notions, as a means to an end.

However, reformism, either for the sake of, or for a means to an end, is not suited for the purposes of Anti-Tech.

This is because we are *not* seeking seats in the government, *nor* a revolution to seize it. We are *not* revolting to embrace a global communist society, *nor* enforcing some 'green radicalism'. There is *no* Anti-Tech Party.

Our goal, as stated above is simply: the abolition of the present technological and economic system, a rebellion against modern civilization.

Anti-Technologists, then, should avoid such activism. Not because we don't believe gay men and women, animals, disabled people and people of color don't deserve the same respect as others, but because such activism does not suit the purposes of an anti-technological revolution.

Reject The Dichotomy

The sins of the Left does not absolve the Right. The Right is dogmatic, hypocritical and equally hating of others. When their idealistic vision of the world is questioned, they become frustrated, too. They want medical and communicative technologies and economic growth. But they also want tradition. You cannot maintain your nation's or tribe's traditions while pushing for technological and economic growth.

Both the Left and the Right are assimilative programmes. As with the current technological and economic system, we should also reject political ideologies of Left and Right. Not in the way fascists are a 'third-way', but we call for a full break from such thinking.

In other words: *Reject the dichotomy, fight for autonomy.*

The (Expansive) Nature of Technology

Neo-Luddism and AP are often subject to the irrational conclusion that technology is unnatural, which in the following section, we will discuss.

(See Ted Kaczynski's *Why the Technological System Will Destroy Itself* for a deeper exploration of the following ideas).

The nature of technology is simply that: a nature. It has functions that are defined by itself, and functions that are influenced by other factors such as the material conditions around it. Very similar to biological organisms like Humans.

Technology, say for example, like capital, is an expanding force. It seeks, by its non-sentient nature, to expand and solve its contradictions. It is a technical evolution, per say. The evolutionary capability of technology does not come from its physical, mechanical aspects. Rather, it comes from two reasons:

1. The development and usage of technologies by institutions (ie, states or corporations)
2. The ideas and social attitudes (myth of progress, rationalization)

1, expanded- If industrial technology was not an efficient method of production, transportation and warfare, it would not be used. It would be weeded out by social evolution, replaced by another system, or perhaps no system may have come close.

2, expanded — Glendinning does put quite well in her manifesto that: "As philosopher Lewis Mumford pointed out, technology consists of more than machines. It includes the techniques of operation and the social organizations that make a particular machine workable. In essence, a technology reflects a worldview. Which particular forms of technology — machines, techniques, and social organizations — are spawned by a particular worldview depends on its perception of life, death, human potential, and the relationship of humans to one another and to nature." For the same reason as point a, if these industrial technology proved unfit to uphold these ideas, it would be rooted out by another system.

These reasons don't show just the ways technology is able to be developed and grow, but it also serves to benefit the reasons. What I mean is that because technology proved efficient for warfare, it allowed advanced militaries to win, and expand, improving their systems as others rose to challenge them. The same can be said for the worldview of progress and rationalism- such ideas influenced the creation of industrial technologies, and those technologies expanded those ideas.

The technological-system and its development can then be understood to be a sort of evolution, as mentioned earlier, placed under evolutionary pressure and forced to adapt, as a biological species would. This is not a conscious choice on the part of the system, just as the evolution to grow legs was not intended by the animals who left the seas.

As such, the development of the system of industrial technology is a natural occurrence of social evolution.

The Bureaucracy of Technology

The Industrial Revolution can be best understood as a factory revolution, based on rationalization, a term we will use often here.

It is best we describe it now:

Rationalization is the method of social and technical organization that places emphasis on: efficiency, predictability, calculability and dehumanization. Such an idea first came from Max Weber, and later expanded upon by thinkers within the Marxian field such as Adorno and Lukács.

Because technology requires and also reinforces a culture of rationality, in the sense we used above, it does so too with bureaucracy.

Weber went to explain how such an organizational discipline emphasizes the need of bureaucracy:

"It is horrible to think that the world could one day be filled with nothing but those little cogs, little men clinging to little jobs and striving towards bigger ones — a state of affairs which is to be seen once more, as in the Egyptian records, playing an ever-increasing part in the spirit of our present administrative system, and especially of its offspring, the students. This passion for bureaucracy ... is enough to drive one to despair. It is as if in politics ... we were deliberately to become men who need "order" and nothing but order, become nervous and cowardly if for one moment this order wavers, and helpless if they are torn away from their total incorporation in it. That the world should know no men but these: it is such an evolution that we are already caught up, and the great question is, therefore, not how we can promote and hasten it, but what can we oppose to this machinery in order to keep a portion of mankind free from this parcelling-out of the soul, from this supreme mastery of the bureaucratic way of life."

For this society to function (which has existed and does now), a knowledgeable group of technicians (those from engineers, programmers, certain politicians and benefactors and so on) must exist to keep the system running, creating dependency on that singular group. A dependency on such a group creates the cog in the machine social order.

Of course, the cog in the machine concept raised here by Weber is one of the greatest examples of the removal of individual dignity. The whole array of technologies and the present economic system could simply not operate if we were to return to an artisan-based society.

What we are speaking on here is not just a political-bureaucracy, but a social-bureaucracy, a fixed state of the individual, bound up in the larger society. And as we have explained above, it is always expanding, meaning, there are less and less places to hide.

This is not to say bureaucracy did not exist before the industrial revolution, but since then, individuals and small-groups are more easily subject to scrutiny from larger organizations, bureaucracy and political leaders. Such methods would include expansive prisons, surveillance systems such as street cameras, and online-monitoring.

Corporations, governments and other organizations (scientific, data collecting, advertising, etc) all take advantage of these processes. Where governments can track our personal experiences, corporations and advertising firms can capitalize on it, for example.

It is also unreasonable to hope all citizens can learn and maintain proper security culture, online and when unplugged. This is because effective methods take dedication and mindfulness and a larger (but perhaps growing?) population do not immediately see the need for such personal security.

'Socialized Technology'

Much of the concerns raised can be attributed to *current* applications of technology, not possible future ones. Communists may raise concerns that industry, capital, commodity production, class societies are the issues — not technology.

While it is true that technology may look radically different under Communism, it is faulty to assume we will know for certain, the functions of such an expansive system.

We can frame it in a way Communists will likely agree with: movements that simply restructure or reorganize capital are not truly revolutionary. The movement may alter the expression of capital, allow it to reorganize and generalize, but it is fundamentally the same.

The same can be said for technology — a restructuring of the system does not necessarily *change* the system's basic properties. Expansion is the largest threat of the system, and perhaps communism, after eliminating the contradictions of producers (proletariat) and exploiters (bourgeoisie), the system may find new ways to expand even faster. It is also possible that after eliminating the profit-motive, technologies may generally speaking, become eco-friendly. Still, we cannot guarantee that outcome and ecological damage is only a part of the larger puzzle.

Who Is The Revolution?

No movement ever succeeded without support from a dedicated and motivated 'base', the larger support, either from fully-formed members or supporters within the masses. These values also should extend to the core, the professional and leading revolutionaries. They should also exemplify values of discipline, unity, dedication, pragmatism, and most importantly, they should be *inspiring*.

The movement needs to develop where the pains of society are most felt, and apply itself to those conditions. The lumpenproletariat *(vagabonds, criminals, prostitutes-* as Marx put it), those living in 'ghettos' or slums, the underpaid factory worker, the illegal immigrant -**those living in the 'shadow' of progress.**

This is not the White Savior complex in the way Modern Leftists are paragons of false virtue for marginalized groups, but in the way Bakunin preached the downtrodden are capable of the highest consciousness.

The privileged bourgeois-minded college kid is not as likely to be *committed* to these ideas, but only appear to be so. (Not to say some bourgeois-minded people won't be useful in their own way.)

Bakunin said of such lower members of society:

that eternal 'meat', [...] that great rabble of the people (underdogs, 'dregs of society') ordinarily designated by Marx and Engels in the picturesque and contemptuous phrase lumpenproletariat. I have in mind the 'riffraff', that 'rabble' almost unpolluted by bourgeois civilization, which carries in its inner being and in its aspirations [...] all the seeds of the socialism of the future...

Of course, we do not claim hold on a socialist future, but rather no future at all, a negation of progress!

Water Seeds, Build Revolutionaries

Early revolutionaries, those who are likely to form the 'core' of the movement-the leaders and major theorists, need to apply themselves to local communities. This means spending time in places that may be alien to them, such as 'slums' or 'ghettos' and put aside one's personal opinions of the locale and the people who live there.

(In reality, if you are repulsed by the people and not the conditions or the larger issues that put them there- you are not wanted in this movement.)

Such starting points may differ, depending on your geography and audience, but you are not there to *save* anyone, you are there to make revolutionaries, to be the gardener of the seed that is in many of them: that of revolution.

Primarily, the 'riffraff' and 'rabble' struggle to stay above just surviving, and many struggle to even make it there. Giving them the resources to build and tend gardens, create community watchmen and so on will allow the revolutionaries an audience. The movement is built, off the shoulders off a beneficial relationship.

I feel the need to say this again: *You are not here to save anyone.*

You are here to guide, and make revolutionaries. Direct their anger, primarily away from 'pseudo-issues' such as immigration, or the liberal-conservative divide. Instead, their minds and hearts should be directed towards techno-industrial society.

Online 'activism', such as debates are no use to us. The major use of the internet should be publications and research, nothing more.

Revolutionary Philosophy And Organization

All actions in the name of the movement, within these local communities and abroad, will alter and manifest as the revolutionaries learn from experience.

In the words of Edward Abbey in his work, *The Monkey Wrench Gang*, "We'll work it out as we go along. Let our practice form our doctrine, thus ensuring precise theoretical coherence" (pg 69).

That being said, should future revolutionaries find what has been laid out above does not manifest in creating revolutionary actions and values, it should be discarded, either in bits or in whole.

On a personal level, *The Revolutionary Catechism* by Sergey Nechayev (1869) should be of heavy influence to members of the movement, especially the 'core' group, the leaders. It outlines, in simple terms, that a revolutionary's primary concern be the revolution itself, becoming almost a manifestation of the movement itself. Nechayev believed the Church, State, etc., operated with violence and amoral character, and to fight these institutions, a revolution should act in the same way to negate these larger forces. We apply the same logic to the Techno-Industrial system.

Of course, the movement's philosophy, its conception of organization and action, should draw on past historical experience: stemming from anarchism first and foremost - and more specifically from its insurrectionist tendencies (from the

Russian Nihilists to the American *galleanisti*, as well as the French illegalists), and accessorily from communist revolutionaries (especially for their vanguardism, self-discipline and emphasis on the importance of dedicated minorities). But we must also look to more contemporary and eclectic examples: such as national liberation guerilla groups, tribal militias or even far-right accelerationists or jihadist fighters.

It should be noted that, just because we find inspiration in some strategic options of Communists and other people with despicable goals does not mean we agree with their overall ideology (ie, Marxism-Leninism, religious bigotry, Nationalism, etc) or actions done in the name of those ideologies. However, we have found that the organizational and disciplinary theories from these groups were/are effective in achieving primary, first goals.

Again, if future revolutionaries find these organizational ideas are not effective, they should be discarded. It is likely we will have to adapt or completely rework our organization, but what was laid out above gives the movement a basic framework, in which to operate from.

A Final Note

The term 'Anti-Tech' (Or the other forms we find it used above) is also used by Kaczynki, but we extend the critique in a more open manner against civilization and metaphysical enslavement (ie, religion, moralism, the state) in ways that compliment the goals at large.

We understand people who have identified with this label before us may not totally agree with our message and expansion of the definition. In all seriousness, we don't care. A label is simply an identifier, and drama around the title is a waste of breath, and obsession over finding a new label is an equal waste of time. Should, down the line, the title of this ideology or any breakaway ideology change, so be it.

This may be a piece I revisit in the future, as the movement and myself evolve. By all means, I am open to criticism on the points presented, especially about organization and philosophy.

I have also chosen to not write in detail, the future of the movement's actions, because I cannot control it, and revolutions are rarely, if at all, subject to predictable cause-and-effect decisions. This is one major issue I see with

Kaczynski's idea of revolution, even if I agree with the larger premises he has laid out.

Such ideas I do agree with are that the system will not likely collapse on its own any time soon, nor will it collapse because of purely revolutionary action. Instead, revolutionaries need to keep a keen eye out for weaknesses, or where the system is struggling. At this point, revolutionaries need to be ready and motivated to kick the legs out from under the system, be it communication systems, power-plants, etc.

***

Violence and the Comanche People

No Noble Savage, No Hobbesian Barbarian

Recommended readings:

Future Primitive: Revisited by John Zerzan.

"Return of the Warrior" & "Atassa: Lessons of the Creek War (1813–1814)" essays in *Atassa. Readings in eco-extremism.*

—

I

The view on violence, and its relation to the Human condition is a divisive one. Historically, the world-builders have believed Humanity is a violent species, greedy and prideful. They believed early, primitive humanity was in a state of barbarism. In the words of Hobbes, primitive life was, "solitary, poor, nasty, brutish, and short" because individuals existed in a state of "..war of all against all." In their own ahistorical understanding, the world-builders believed social contracts were formed, bringing about a more stable society, what we call civilization (especially in a Eurocentric understanding). Ironically, such stable societies have created, out of necessity, unique social regulators like ever growing laws and religious institutions (Judaism, Hinduism, Buddhism, Christianity, Islam..) that help us understand the human condition and keep the peace. See the Christian view:

For from within, out of the heart of man, come evil thoughts, sexual immorality, theft, murder, adultery, coveting, wickedness, deceit, sensuality, envy, slander, pride, foolishness. All these evil things come from within, and they defile a person.
Mark 7: 21–23

However, there has been a tendency in anthropology circles since the 1960's that has countered this view: That early Homos, since their split with their more violent Chimpanzee cousins, were an example of affluence, little to moderate violence, and social equity that stands in contrast to modern society. One pioneer of this anthropological revolution was/is Marshall Sahlins, with his work, *The*

Original Affluent Society. We've also begun to understand since then, especially with the popularization of Marxian history, that mass societies were not a peaceful development, but one born from violence and coercion. Read *The Origin of the Family, Private Property and the State* by Friedrich Engels. Even before this, there was Jean-Jacques Rousseau, ideological enemy to Hobbes who stated, "Man is born free and everywhere he is in chains."

As the debate on violence continues, anti-civilization circles must try to break with the Noble Savage analysis, as seen in my Zerzan suggested reading; but take care not to be edgy contrarians and adopt the Hobbesian view, which is but a World-Builder ideology, one that comes through in the first suggested *Atassa* reading I have included.

There is instead, a 'spectrum' of sorts. It wasn't that one day, groups of humans woke up with new views on violence and waged war for their neighbor's land and trading materials; on the other hand, to believe humans are "naturally" and unconditionally peaceful is simply untrue. For example, the Comanche people were in near constant conflict (endemic conflict), but the values and goals represented what some like myself consider a middle-path of the development of mass-violence. For the bulk of this essay, we will examine the Comanche people and their relationship to violence in hopes of breaking from the dogmatic view of humanity's capacity for violence.

II

The Comanche were a nomadic people, who lacked any true central governing body. Instead, they had ever developing 'divisions', which can be understood as affinity tribes. The divisions were largely built on common interests such as trade, peace-making, and war. The Comanche were reliant primarily on hunting, trading, and raiding. The hunting provided basic subsistence for them, as they were a nomadic people. To understand the importance of trading and raiding within the Comanche way of life, one must understand that the Comanche identity was based within horses, and thus, ventures of trade and raids centered on obtaining more horses.

One may argue then that wealth was the center of what violence the Comanche had initiated, but I'd argue differently. Wealth here was an individual's wealth, and his prestige. In fact, a man's wealth was often measured by the size of his horse herd, and young boys were even taught to ride before they could even walk — further showing the cultural and economic importance of the horse in the Comanche way of life. It is important to also understand the horses' relation to the male-female relations in the Comanche way of life, as it strengthened the division of labor. Women did not have access to horses, and already were confined to 'home-life' typical of institutional divisions of labor.

Wealth and the social view of greed in Comanche society was similar to many pre-agricultural societies, with a hoarding of most forms of wealth being looked down upon. Material wealth and other possessions were often discarded upon death of the owner, much like their neighbors, the Kiowa. Not only this, but possessions were given up during a 'Give-Away' ritual, where a young man had his coming of age and was announced as a warrior. Members of the band would offer up most, if not all, of their own belongings to the larger community during these rituals. This was common across the Plains Indians, and could almost be considered a rule of thumb for all nomadic and semi-nomadic indigenous people of 'America.'

It is important to understand the view of wealth in these societies, because of the actual use of it. Since horses were a tool for hunting, war, and travel, the wealth here is tangible and visible, it has human use. It is not like the flow of Capital in our industrial era, which acts as a mediator of relations. Violence, then, is a way of accumulating wealth and possessions that had use-value. This is further supported in the specific case of the Comanche, who's raids were almost entirely focused on obtaining horses, sometimes numbering in the hundreds.

Another important note is that the accumulation of wealth here, that of a communal wealth, is not quite easy to compare to those of modern nations. The fluid change of hands, and use-values represent their own ends, while wealth accumulation is a means to mediation and representation of Capital in industrial nations.

However, we must note that this accumulation is also based in the domestication process. Were it not for horses, and the Comanche's relation to other domesticators, logically their wealth and possessions would look radically different; more so comparable to hunter-gatherer proper, whose wealth was truly negligible. This is especially true with the growing trade with European powers. As their relation to the colonists grew, so did the Comanche range of influence. A self serving cycle.

III

The other point of violence to be discussed is one's sense of identity. I don't mean identity in some larger-than-life ethnic construction. What I mean is one's identity in their day to day life, and their self-realization through communal life. This could manifest in conflict with other inidigenous peoples, but I wish to focus on their anti-colonial struggles, the Comanche Wars, specifically.

In defense of their way of life, and the corresponding natural terrain, the Comanche held the region commonly called Comancheria, Comanchería, or Nʉmʉnʉʉ Sookobitʉ (Comanche land). This region spanned a large portion of modern day New Mexico, west Texas, and parts of Colorado, Oklahoma and Kansas. Conflict was between the Comanche and Spanish, Mexicans and Americans, depending on the time.

Interestingly, disease, at first, failed to weaken the Comanche forces, but groups like the Apache were hit hard, and this allowed the Comanche to expand influence over the region. Some have come to call this phenomenon empire building, which I disagree with on the basis they expanded not by conquest, but because competition had left, died off, or assimilated into the Comanche.

However, drought eventually began to weaken this 'empire', which had also begun to expand into Mexico for resources, specifically horses. With this drought, diseases finally began to overtake the Comanche people. This weakening prompted the local non-indigenous forces to attack. Fast moving raids on forts and settlements proved to be the Comanchean solution. Assisted by horses, they began to be seen as the strongest cavalry in the world, and gained the title of "Lords of the Plains." One such raid was the Fort Parker Massacre, where Comanche and allied indigenous peoples attacked a pioneer family, the Parkers. Several children were taken and either sold or assimilated into Comanchean culture. The most famous, Cynthia Ann Parker, a nine-year old girl was taken into her captors' culture. There, she lived with them for 25 years and married to Peta Nocona, a chief of the Nokoni band.

With Peta, Cynthia produced three children, one of them being the last chief before the Comanche were placed into reservations. She was brought back to Anglo society after her band was attacked by United States Texas Rangers. She even attempted to return to the Comanche years later, but was brought back to her home. She failed to reintegrate and eventually died of self-induced starvation after her daughter passed of influenza.

There is much to be said of Cynthia choosing to live among the Comanche, and grieving the times long past, failing to return to her parent culture in a healthy way. She was not the only one of this case, and her brother had a similar fate.

Returning to the main point: in fact of extinction, or assimilation, the Comanche chose conflict, violence against pioneers who encroached on their land. In what may be seen as hypocrisy, Comanche continued to trade with any and all who would benefit them, even if some of the population (Divisions) were at war with their trading partners. However, an interesting point can be made on this observation: the reason the Comanche never developed mass society and through this, mass violence, was because their culture lacked any concrete central governing body to represent the whole of the people. Instead, the Divisions, these affinity tribes, functioned by common interest, not coercion.

IV

What does this rambling history lesson mean for the anti-civilization, eco-extremist, primitivist milieu? Not much, if one continues to believe violence is a law of civilization alone. It also will mean something radically different for those who perhaps worship, or revere violence. I hope that these circles embrace a more nuanced understanding of violence beyond the typical Leftist "class war."

Phenomenologically speaking, war of pacification and assimilation, ie, violence by the State, or within a larger framework of what we call (industrial) civilization is radically different than "democratic" war of prestige and identity within tribal contexts. Individualist anarchism of Europe pioneered a sort of way of discerning violence of the individual and that of the State/Society, and perhaps we need to revisit that mentality in a 21st century anti-civilization context. I personally do not believe myself to be the one to define that, only to help begin the dialogue by analyzing historical trends of violence in relation to social structures.

***

What Is Home?

A Short Anthropological Overview of Paleolithic Shelter

So-called neighborhood crime watch (ie, snitches) and a faltering sense of community* are but a few symptoms of the decay of the idyllic cul-de-sac image. Today, your neighborhood is a method of monitoring, with doorbell and driveway cameras. A sense of community in one's neighborhood is quickly draining away. I often hear those older than me reflect when it was much more common to walk over to the neighbor's house for dinner or a movie, with parents talking and children playing. Cookouts, yard sales as social events, scavenger hunts are events I remember as much more common events from my own childhood (I am only 23, for reference).

Is this because of the rise of « neoliberalism », a decay of moral values, home development plans or something else? How far back does the issue at hand go? What caused it? Without giving an elaborate history of neighborhoods and capitalist home design, I want to explore the ethos and strategies of shelter building in the Paleolithic, to be read alongside the likes of *The City and its Inmates* by John Zerzan. This text is limited in scope, because originally, it was intended as a shorter polemic, but quickly transformed into an anthropological examination of an often unattended topic, to show there is an alternative to the current system, albeit in a very focused manner.

‒‒‒

In 2018, I contributed to the *Ultra Left International: A Manifesto*. One of my most important contributions was a small one, a footnote that became a sentence within the work itself, "Even under primitive communism alienation from the natural world was arguably the seed which evolved into societal alienation."

While I now hold a differing view, that Ritual was the birth of social alienation, I think that this notion of separateness has stuck with me for a while because I keep finding others have a similar view of separation, including the physical, spiritual and the psychological manifestations of it. It makes my understanding of the apparent decay of social relations more clear.

Fredy Perlman, in his *Against His-Story, Against Leviathan,* wrote:

Those who wall themselves in fall into a similar trap [self-defeat, my note].

Communities built walls before, at Jericho for example. But they built a wall once. Wall-building was not an institution among them. [...] Jericho's walls will no longer do. The walls have to be high and strong, and they have to be repaired as often as the ditches of Erech. [..] The seasons pass and the generations pass, yet the walls must still be maintained. And maintained they are, generation after generation. [...] Walls cannot be permanently maintained with a temporary division of labor.

I don't write this with the intent to speak extensively of the ills of urbanization and cities. That much is self-evident within the Anti-Civilization milieu (or at least, I hope so, as some individuals try very hard to "synthesize," and or otherwise bring about nonsense). What I wish to speak about is the formation of physical separation before cities. What I mean is the enclosed living space and how we got here.

The development of enclosed living spaces has within it the nucleus of separation that we continue to perpetuate today, as described above. What I mean when I say enclosed living space is a more permanent shelter in which only a section of the wider community (immediate or near-immediate family, roommates, a single individual, etc) is housed. These buildings also tend to rely on a division of labor and later, resources from abroad. Houses, apartments, and condos are contemporary examples. I contrast this with the existence of shelters in the Paleolithic that I define as temporary, encompassing a large portion of a foraging community, and based on the resources from the immediate environment. Such examples will be discussed below.

The most popular conception of Paleolithic shelter is, of course, the cave. However, while there is consensus on humans using caves as shelters, the amount of caves would never have housed the existing numbers of ancient Humans (of which I mean species ranging from *H. Erectus* to *H. Sapiens*). So, while understanding caves were important for the Human family, especially when leaving our native Africa, I will focus on built structures. Also, these are not Human-made structures, and are at best, altered to suit more comfortable living.

Of course, a suburban home is hardly comparable to a living space like that possibly found in Terra Amata, France some 400,000 years ago. This contested site showed evidence of fire hearths within a space made of wooden poles and even animal skins, possibly housing twenty to forty people at once. That number would represent a large portion of a band, that of *Homo Erectus* or *Heidelbergensis*, which had a median community size of 50–100. While it is disputed if this was indeed a shelter (as opposed to natural placement of these materials by wind and water), reconstruction images show it would have had an open space as an entrance, a welcoming and non-enclosed space (excluding a possibility of a cover for the entrance).

Living spaces such as Neanderthal-made mammoth bone shelters are a similar example. A Ukrainian site was the site of a shelter described as, "The home was apparently built in two parts. The lower part, or base, was made by assembling large mammoth bones to support the whole structure, which was 26 feet across at its widest. The bones themselves were likely obtained both through collecting those found on the ground and by killing the large beasts directly themselves."A similar find in Siberia, also made by Neanderthals, was indicative of housing *several* families, by the presence of several small hearths. This is even more interesting by the fact that Neanderthals had smaller communities than compared to us.

In addition to what I define as a typical Paleolithic shelter, is that when they were left behind, these shelters would simply fall apart and decompose or some parts may have even been recycled, hence the little evidence until later in the archeological record. The ethos and characteristics of these shelters are extensions of the foraging way of life. A South African history site the San of the Stone Age describes their shelter practices in a similar way, "[They] did not live in permanent houses, but in shelters made of materials they could find around them, like thin branches and tall grass. […] They never settled in the same campsite, but used the same waterholes as they moved around. This also ensured that the land did not become exhausted."

After the move out of Africa, and the extensive use of new environments, the use of caves in relation to Human-made shelters likely would be lower, especially as I said, caves could not support the relatively low Human populations. Is the decrease in cave habitation and other uses for survival a reason we find evidence of Ritual-Art in them? In fact, evidence for cave habitation in the Upper Paleolithic decreases and it is only in this time period that we find evidence of Ritual! Is this because our mental association with caves and rock shelters had faded and instead been used for Ritual because of a need for space to express Symbolic behavior, both in Art and more advanced forms of burial? Perhaps, since Ritual is an act that is disconnected from the day to day lives of individuals.

Locations in the Upper Paleolithic begin to take on the role of sanctuary, with man-made structures exhibit ritual affairs, too, such as elaborate disposal of dead group members. Perhaps there is a link of separateness between the building of more complex (still not housing, per say) campsite shelters and the Ritual mediation we know developed in the Upper Paleolithic? This would line up with the writing of Chris Scarre who states that less ambiguous evidence for shelters appears after 50,000 years ago. Scarre states these "more substantial structures" contrast with the earlier "flimsy" shelters of the Lower and Middle Paleolithic. The importance of the date is that this aligns with the so-called Behavioral Revolution, which brought about an explosion of symbolic expression, such as Ritual and art. Echoing upcoming Neolithic and even modern housing is evidence of multi-room structures in the Upper Paleolithic as well.

There truly is no place like home, when Earth itself is recognized as the home.

* I remember a Real Estate website stating, "Neighbors aren't as friendly as before due to changes in lifestyle and technological advancements that have reduced social interaction and made many less open to meeting others." The fast paced, online experience of modern life is so visible, yet never criticized by many...

***

***

Regional Collapse, Regional Liberation

or: The Primitivist Theory of Combined & Uneven Development

Introduction

The spread of Capitalism and Industrialism was predominantly a 'Western' phenomenon, which slowly disseminated among the world through trade, and colonial and imperial relations.

The centers of industrial-economics, or the First World, outsources the process of primary industry — the extraction and collection of natural resources to the Third World. The First World then takes this industry and turns it into secondary industry — the goods themselves- manufacturing.

With the expansion of decentralized production, we see a more efficient system of the development of technologies and general goods in the First World, while the Third World provides the basis for that system. It is no secret that the Third World is under the systems of neo-colonialism and imperialism, their labor and resources extracted at an unfair, and uneven rate. This creates a hierarchical system of power, creating an interesting situation in the fight against Industry: If civilization and industry did not come across the world evenly, then we cannot expect the collapse to act in such a linear, immediate manner.

Historical Precedence

In the words of Leon Trotsky, "...[T]he entire history of mankind is governed by the law of uneven development." Trotsky saw development as uneven, meaning the world does not progress at the same pace, either through economic developments or cultural norms. It also would include secondary characteristics such as population density.

Even within a single state, we can see developments that do not progress equally. The greatest example is the North-South divide of the United States. Where the North embraced and grew under the Industrial Revolution, limiting the need for slave labor, in exchange for a wage system; the South kept a primarily agrarian economy, relying more so on slave labor and plantation systems.

However, the North and South were of course not isolated from one another, but had constant relations, positive and negative. The North was able to finance their industrialization through taxes on imports, many of which impacted the South more so than the North.

Besides the North favoring an industrial, free-market economy, and the South's preference of agrarian slavery; the cityscape and transportation methods were vastly different, due to the factors of economic differences.

Industrialism allowed the North to enlarge their urban areas. The North's largest cities in 1860 were New York City and Philadelphia, whose populations were roughly 813,669 and 565,529, respectively. Contrast this to the South in the same year, whose largest cities were New Orleans and Charleston, with populations at 168,675 and 40,522, respectively. The North's two largest cities as listed alone added to 1,379,198 and the South's added only to 209,197. Only one-tenth of Southerners lived in urban areas, while the North held one-quarter in their urban areas.

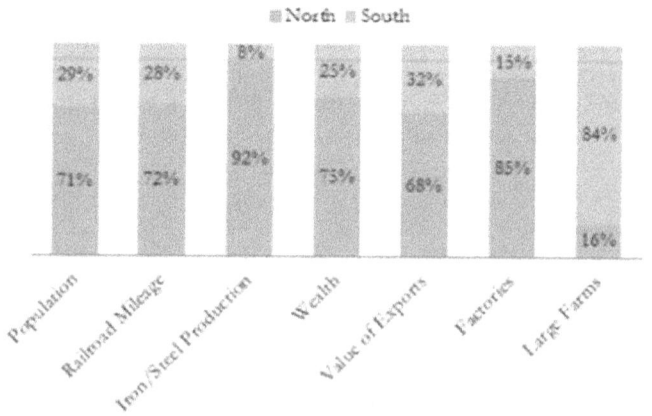

I found some varying reports on this information, but this seemed the most consistent—from battlefields.org

The North also held over 7/10ths of all railroads, allowing a growing effective method transportation of both people and goods. This also served important during the Civil War. In contrast, the South utilized horse-drawn carriages and steamboats more often.

Perhaps another example of this theory of development can be shown, but more on the side of 'combined' rather than 'uneven'. For this, I will cite two passages from Trotsky, the main proponent of the theory:

"The meagerness not only of Russian feudalism, but of all the old Russian history, finds its most depressing expression in the absence of real mediaeval cities as centres of commerce and craft. Handicraft did not succeed in Russia in separating itself from agriculture, but preserved its character of home industry. The old Russian cities were commercial, administrative, military and manorial — centres of consumption, consequently, not of production.. Even Novgorod, similar to Hansa and not subdued by the Tartars, was only a commercial, and not an industrial city. True, the distribution of the peasant industries over various districts created a demand for trade mediation on a large scale. But nomad traders could not possibly occupy that place in social life which belonged in the West to the craft-guild and merchant-industrial petty and middle bourgeoisie, inseparably bound up with its peasant environment. The chief roads of Russian trade, moreover, led across the border, thus from time immemorial giving the leadership to foreign commercial capital, and imparting a semi-colonial character to the whole process, in which the Russian trader was a mediator between the Western cities and the Russian villages. This kind of economic relation developed further during the epoch of Russian capitalism and found its extreme expression in the imperialist war[...] The law of combined development reveals itself most indubitably, however, in the history and character of Russian industry. Arising late, Russian industry did not repeat the development of the advanced countries, but inserted itself into this development, adapting their latest achievements to its own backwardness. Just as the economic evolution of Russia as a whole skipped over the epoch of craft-guilds and manufacture, so also the separate branches of industry made a series of special leaps over technical productive stages that had been measured in the West by decades. Thanks to this, Russian industry developed at certain periods with extraordinary speed. Between the first revolution and the war, industrial production in Russia approximately doubled. This has seemed to certain Russian historians a sufficient basis for concluding that "we must abandon the legend of backwardness and slow growth." In reality the possibility of this swift growth was determined by that very backwardness which, alas, continued not only up to the moment of liquidation of the old Russia, but as her legacy up to the present day."

As Trotsky explained, Russia's unique development was largely due to Russia's relation to Western Europe through foreign financing, which can be seen as a growth retarder and a semi-colonial oppression. This led to a mix of Russia's 'backwardness' (feudal relations) and industry (from the West). It did not develop on its own, but rather, was inserted into its condition, as Trotsky stated.

Interestingly, the United States also had its own combined development, as it had skipped the stage of feudalism. Instead, it was born among competing Western nations, predominantly France and Britain in the later years. While it did begin mostly as an agrarian nation, it did not have the 'tributary' aspects of Feudalism. This may be an explanation for the North-South economic divide. Also, the historically large amount of slave labor, shared by the North and South, may have also been caused by this — as it had not developed its own cultural economic identity.

Compressions and Descalings

The progression of technology and culture has not developed on a linear path, but rather a complex series of 'compressions' and 'descalings'. A compression (or acceleration) is seen in developing countries' pseudo-industrial developments paired with their more tribal or primitive social organization. A descaling is more in-line with the fall of political, economic and/or technological capabilities of the post-Soviet states.

Compressions and Descalings can come in different intensities. For example, the descalings of the post-Soviet states is hardly comparable to the situation in which Western Rome fell into smaller Nation-States. The Soviet Union, under the NEP and the 5-year plans of Lenin and Stalin respectively, accelerated scientific; technological; agricultural; and cultural developments under the influence of their respective systems, but also due to relations to other countries. The Soviet Union, despite holding contrarian ideology, held trade and service relations to countries like the United States, Canada and Western Europe. This could include bartering products, hiring foreign construction and engineering firms, and standard credit/cash-for-product trade.

These relations, especially under the first two 5-Year plans between 1928–1937, compressed or rather, accelerated the Soviet industrial system.

Exploitation

While the Soviet Union benefited heavily from these accelerations, other countries do not. Russia before the Bolsheviks had a semi-colonial relation to Western Europe; today, areas of Asia, South America and Africa have similar relations to pre-Bolshevik Russia. It creates a culture where these developing, exploited countries are "inserted…into this development, adapting [the West's] latest achievements to its own backwardness."

These countries are victims of exploitation such as neo-colonialism and imperialism. They are given foreign aid; machinery; and corporate and political influence from the West *only as long* as they use it to benefit their oh so benevolent benefactors.

With the growing environmental crisis, there will be a larger and larger cause for 'green' and 'sustainable' technology. Such issues from this includes the health issues from producing Silicon, impacting both miners and the environment. Silicon is currently the most popular material in Solar Cells.

But health issues are the least of our worries, especially in the developed world, where health and work codes are most advanced. Istead, it is the Developing World — where the highest price has been paid for humanity's rare mineral addiction.

Take the Democratic Republic of Congo, where 60% of cobalt, a material popular in batteries. Excessive human rights abuses, child labor and environmental negligence have been birthed by the growing market for cobalt, especially under the guise of electric vehicles. Colton's main producers are Rwanda, the Democratic Republic of the Congo, Nigeria, Brazil and China, and this production has constantly stirred what can be called 'Colton Ethics'. Almost all the listed countries have been accused of human rights and child labor abuse, either in the extraction or processing of the materials, according to the ILRF. Colton of course is used primarily in smartphones and computers, a large 'necessity' in today's day-to-day life.

Copper and cobalt mine, DRC

Many companies like Apple only temporarily ceased buying materials from countries like Democratic Republic of Congo after large report of 'slave conditions' was released in 2016 and 2017, despite smaller reports repeating the same horrid information years prior. Apple has even moved to purchase those materials from China, despite having their own disastrous human-rights and ecological issues. China even has their hands in the DRC, so this is more a round-about purchase than benevolent market decisions on the side of Apple and others. So evidently, this growing Green Revolution is not as sustainable as one may believe.

Some may make the case for Socialist or Communist relations as a solution to this exploitation, but there simply is a lack of evidence to show the end of capital is the end of all exploitation. Citing Marx and Co. as prophets is only an appeal to authority, not an analysis of previous socialist experiments or 'post-Socialist' states.

Regional Collapse

The above mentioned information may very well seem irrelevant to the Primitivist movement, and more in line with Communist rhetoric, and this is true. Most talk of exploitation is associated with a critique of class society than technology, unless it means as a general rule of thumb of the common person.

However, this does not mean we cannot adopt Communist analysis for our means. It also gives us the basis of a more realistic analysis. Where many Primitivists (such as Kaczynski) see a total collapse (either quickly or over a period of time) as feasible, other Primitivists such as myself and Jacobi instead push for the idea of "regional collapse."

This is not to say we dismiss the idea of a total civilizational collapse, or don't want it, but we don't see it as necessarily realistic. If we understand the rise of civilization, agriculture, capital and technology as uneven, and sometimes in completely isolated areas, how can we expect the collapse of industrial / world society to be some sort of global apocalypse? We can't.

While globalism expands via increasingly effective methods of travel and communication, we may very well see domino effects — a truly crippling strike can indeed cause a rapid collapse, but an apocalyptic worldview is more cinematic than realistic. The timescale of such a collapse will indeed be quick in a historical sense. For example, Rome's collapse was a collection of mass diseases, financial issues, infighting for power, incompetent leaders and a total complexity that far outweighed any available energy (food, manpower, technology). These collective issues spanned almost 300 years until Rome's *total* collapse between 476–480.

By regional collapse, we essentially mean regions of varying sizes and cultural diversity will see localized movements against industrial / world society. These movements may or may not share our ideological views. But, whether or not they mean to, they are fighting against industrial/world Society. Religious fundamentalism, tribal conflict against larger nations and so forth are examples. This method of revolution, of course, is a sort of balkanization.

We can see inspiration in movements that base their seizure of power through balkanization, such as the Zaptasitas. In the words of John Jacobi:

The Zapatistas, of course, are the most obvious example of the latter. In the 90s they utilized new internet technologies and the political power of NGOs to win a sufficient amount of territory for their social ideals. They survive to this day, and have, in most respects, won. Not nearly enough to challenge industrial society, they are nevertheless representative of the kind of balkanization we should like to see in the future.

Furthermore, Jacobi said:

Even since 2001 there have been a number of revolutions, successful insurgent struggles, and related radical political events. That these are only regional supports the author's contention that revolutionary struggle alone cannot solve the global ecological crisis, but there is no reason to dispose of regionally-confined revolutions as a tool in our toolkit. It is entirely feasible to imagine ecologically-based social transformation happening through a series of revolutions, just as Enlightenment ideas started in France, spread to the rest of Europe through Napoleon, and eventually made it to the New World with the American revolutionaries and Simon Bolivar.

And finally:

But if the preservation of traditional communities and the collapse of industrial infrastructure is to be assured, we will need to figure out a way to mobilize these regional phenomena for an offensive against industrial society.

These regional collapses or balkanizations are extreme examples of the above mentioned descalings, with massive implications in all regards. What is needed is a mobilization and critical support of these movements under our ideological framework. What these specifics will be, are beyond us at this time.

In addition, the continued exploitation, unless solved in the near future, will continue to create situations of conflict, mostly those with many parties involved, and with new rules of engagement.

Jean Baudrillard best put this as, *"Today's terrorism is not the product of a traditional history of anarchism, nihilism, or fanaticism. It is instead the contemporary partner of globalization."*

Regional Liberation

With our proceeding statements of regional collapse, descalings and uneven development leading to exploitation, we have come to the last major point in this piece — our support for regional liberation. This has heavy similarities to the Leninist conception of National Liberation — where a nation has the right to fight against colonial or imperial powers in order to define their own destiny in terms of socialist development.

However, of course our support comes from challenging the stability of regions, economically and politically. With the rise of multi-party conflicts in exploited nations and semi-colonies, at home and abroad, there is a possible future of Primitivist support and even influence in these events.

Of course, not all regional movements will necessarily benefit us. However, tribal insurgencies, national movements, religious uprising, anti-Western demonstrations all are possible events in which we can place our critical support or even assert possible influence, either through a future, above ground movement; or disseminate our ideology through other, secret methods.

Typically the regional liberation side of balkanization will likely exist in the Developing world, or areas within developed nations that are 'backwater'. For example, in China, the peasants stand in stark contrast to the urban centers. In America, share-cropping exists in its own contrast to Western development.

Otherwise, balkanization movements, either with politics that are Primitivist or not — will have their own reasons. These may be a result of political turmoil, desertification or other destabilizing events.

Our goal should be to bring these movements under a larger movement, or political identity. If not, our support for them will be crucial. Global crime, terrorism and war will be our situational allies. Paring with other political and/or religious radicals, and tribal or oppressed national groups, especially those already involved with their own conflicts, will be of good use in our toolkit.

Federation of American Scientists published a piece in 1996 titled 'Global Organized Crime' and the following selection makes an interesting point:

[...] Many terrorist groups that engage in violent acts are motivated by specific political causes, such as Egyptian Islamic Fundamentalist terrorists who use violent means to protest their country's current government and Western influences, most organized crime groups are only interested in political power for the security it would provide their organization and are primarily motivated by money.

The international economic threat, posed by Global Organized Crime, in an increasingly global economy is among the major "new" threats to national security. The major economic powers and the less developed nations did not previously share a collective problem of this nature. Global Organized Crime does not just affect a select group of financial institutions or regional areas, it affects international financial networks and economies at a national level.

The author believed such Global Organized Crime threatens our global economy and political structures, global and national:

Transnational organized crime groups pose more of a threat to international financial markets as the world economy becomes increasingly interdependent. Laundering billions of dollars in organized crime money worsens national debt problems because the large sums of money are then lost as tax revenue to that country's government.

Global Organized Crime can have a damaging effect on political structures, especially the fragile new systems of government found in the former communist or totalitarian regimes. South American drug cartels have a destabilizing effect on governments through their financial support of local guerilla rebels, such as the Sendero Luminoso in Peru and the Revolutionary Armed Forces in Columbia, who share their animosity toward the government and who exchange protection for money and arms supplies. The Sicilian Mafia have used their economic power over local businesses and banks and their supplies of cash to corrupt politicians, judges and Law Enforcement, assassinating many of those public figures who will not cooperate. Media polls indicate that the many Russians believe the "mafiya" is more powerful than the government. As people feel that the government is powerless to stop organized crime, they turn to crime leaders for protection and political institutions begin to deteriorate. Fear of organized crime undermines the credibility of political reform and may encourage support for anti-democratic, hardline politicians such as Russia's Vladimir Zhirinovsky who promised during the 1993 campaign to end organized crime in 3 months through mass arrest and execution.

The global networks of criminals, terrorists and corrupt government officials and their complex methods of smuggling goods could easily be transferred to the smuggling of nuclear materials on a massive scale. While Global Organized Crime has become increasingly more involved in the transfer of arms, encouraged in part by conflicts in the Balkans and former Soviet Union which proved to be profitable for the Russian and Italian mafia, the smuggling of nuclear materials seems to be currently isolated to select incidents and mostly to amateurs. Russia no longer has the nuclear materials protection that it had during the Cold War when materials were controlled by a tight, centralized system under a politically powerful government. In the past year, the FBI has seized major shipments of nuclear materials in Eastern Europe, including large seizures of cesium in Lithuania and uranium in the Czech Republic. As Global Organized Crime groups become more powerful and as nuclear materials become more vulnerable (through poor management, underpaid desperate workers in the nuclear facilities, and government corruption) the threat becomes more serious.

International drug trafficking poses a threat to the social fabric of all countries. The increase in the scale of these operations has led to an increase in drug use, addiction, and general crime level. The common U.S.-Mexico border alone causes a tremendous increase in the American drug problem: 60–70% of cocaine in the U.S. enters at this border through a Mexican-Columbian organized crime partnership. Other European organized crime groups use this border to transport heroin, marijuana, and methamphetamine. It is becoming increasingly difficult to track the flow of narcotics into the United States as the drug cartel methods become more technically sophisticated: redesigning the interiors of Boeing 727s to hold maximum amounts of cocaine; transferring drug profits electronically to dozens of banks around the world in less than 24 hours; and using falsified export documents and invoices for goods in order to disguise drug trafficking transactions.

So not everyone who will be contributing to the balkanization of society will have ideological motivations: some will simply be in it for self-motivation, weather that be in relation to religious loyalties, or community, or money. But because these interests naturally clash with the dominant society, they function well as a source of radical political energy and potential.

A Final Note

While the above mentioned theories have basis in Marxist, Communist and Far-Left analysis, I by no means agree with their overall goals. Primitivism as a semi-coherent ideology is still young and absolutely should look to a plethora of other, history-tested ideologies to supplement itself.

As always, the ideas and theories presented here will continue to be tested as Primitivism spreads and is challenged. At no point will I ever imply my ideas are set in stone, or my theories are immortal. I hope for my ideas to be challenged, both in discourse and in action.

For Wildness,

A.G.T.

Contact:

Email: *wildmanspath@protonmail.com*

Twitter: *@tribalreaction*

*